better together*

*This book is best read together, grownup and kid.

a kids book about allyship

by Rebecca Gitlitz-Rapoport
and Sam Rapoport

A Kids Co.
Editor Emma Wolf
Designer Rick DeLucco
Creative Director Rick DeLucco
Studio Manager Kenya Feldes
Sales Director Melanie Wilkins
Head of Books Jennifer Goldstein
CEO and Founder Jelani Memory

DK
Delhi Technical Team Bimlesh Tiwary Pushpak Tyagi, Rakesh Kumar
Senior Production Editor Jennifer Murray
Senior Production Controller Louise Minihane
Senior Acquisitions Editor Katy Flint
Acquisitions Project Editor Sara Forster
Managing Art Editor Vicky Short
Managing Director, Licensing Mark Searle

First American edition, 2025
Published in the United States by DK Publishing, 1745 Broadway, 20th Floor,
New York, NY 10019

First published in Great Britain in 2025 by
Dorling Kindersley Limited, 20 Vauxhall Bridge Road, London SW1V 2SA
A Penguin Random House Company

The authorised representative in the EEA is
Dorling Kindersley Verlag GmbH. Arnulfstr. 124, 80636 Munich, Germany

A catalog record for this book is available from the Library of Congress.
A CIP catalogue record for this book is available from the British Library.
ISBN: 978-0-2417-4356-0

DK books are available at special discounts when purchased in bulk for sales
promotions, premiums, fund-raising, or education use. For details, contact:
DK Publishing Special Markets, 1745 Broadway, 20th Floor, New York, NY 10019
SpecialSales@dk.com

Printed and bound in China
www.dk.com
akidsco.com

MIX
Paper | Supporting
responsible forestry
FSC™ C018179

This book was made with Forest
Stewardship Council™ certified
paper – one small step in DK's
commitment to a sustainable future.
**Learn more at www.dk.com/uk/
information/sustainability**

This book is for all the kids who stand up and take risks for other kids.

And to our kids, Jordy and Tobin: buckle up! We'll be on this journey as a family forever.

Intro
for grownups

We all want the kids in our lives to stand up for what's right. We want them to feel empowered to stop the bullies, be inclusive with their friends, and to speak up when they see something that isn't right.

Hopefully, as kids become grownups themselves, our teachings will turn into actions like stopping those who interrupt people during meetings, amplifying the voices of the unheard or ignored, and pushing back on offensive comments or jokes.

These choices seem simple enough. So why are they so hard to carry out?

This book will empower kids to be allies now so they can use this important skill for the rest of their lives. We truly believe empowering our kids with this superpower can change the world.

Have you ever heard the word...

ally?

An ally is something everyone needs,

An ally is something everyone can be,

It feels good to have one,

Want to learn more?

but not everyone has.

but not everyone is.

it feels good to be one.

we've got you!

Hi. We're Sam and Becca.

We're married.

We're gay.

We're parents to 2 kids.

And we are on a magical journey to be better allies.

The thing is, allyship *isn't* magic.

It's really all about

learning,

respecting,

listening,

and most
importantly— acting.

So then what is allyship?

Very simply, allyship is noticing problems wherever they are and being a part of the solutions, even when it's hard.

But being an ally is so much more than that.

To us, allyship is...

getting involved when
things don't seem right.

speaking out against unfairness,
even when it's scary to do so.

showing up for people
who are often left out.

encouraging people to share
their stories, and believing them,
even if you don't understand.

being OK with feeling
uncomfortable.

learning from your mistakes.

knowing it takes a
lifelong commitment.

We are allies when...

we support and
celebrate the things that
make us all unique.

We all have

differ

ences!

In this world, some of us are:

shy people

loud people

white people

asian people

people

people who wear glasses

people who are women

people who are asian and Black

people who are men

transgender people

Black people

Latinx people

Middle Eastern people

people who use a wheelchair

people who are deaf and gay.

All these identities
create so many perspectives,
cultures, foods, writing,
music, and stories.

The more we support
this diversity through allyship,
the more incredible the world is.

It's true!

Now think about the
kids at your school.

Does every person in your class have the same number of friends?

Do some people get treated differently because of who their parents are?

Do they all get celebrated or corrected by your teacher the same way?

Does everyone get picked for teams fairly?

Have you ever seen someone get made fun of because of the way they look or act?

Even though the 2 of us
know the world is so much better
when we celebrate other people
and everything that makes them
special, it doesn't always happen
like that in real life.

Sometimes people don't accept others who are different from what they're used to.

Or they've been told only a certain kind of people are the *right kind* of people.

Some groups of people
are more often treated unfairly.

They are made to feel like

outsiders.

How does that

make you feel?

Now imagine if your best friend
were being treated unfairly
just for being who they are.

Maybe they feel like people don't want to be their friend, and so they stop having fun and start feeling really sad.

You wouldn't want that
for your friend, would you?

**Would you want *anyone*
to feel that way?**

That's where being an ally starts:
seeing something happen
and knowing it's not right.

Next, you actually
do something about it.

To help you take action, we've created a list of important things to remember.

Turn the page and let's begin.

How to start becoming an ally:

listen.

When you listen, you hear the story of someone's life no matter what they're talking about—their family, favorite sport, or maybe their favorite music.

When you listen, you empower the people who are talking and you learn from those around you.

learn.

We all know our own lives the best.

We can better understand the world we share by learning from people who are different from us.

Respect.

It's not always easy to talk about yourself, and when someone feels open enough to do so, trust their story, even if you don't understand it.

advocate.

Stand up and speak out for others, even when you feel scared to do so, whether a lot of people are watching or no one is.

Be willing to give something up.

As an ally, you might lose a friend or get made fun of, and that can hurt.

But doing what's right for others sometimes means you lose something yourself.

accept feedback.

If someone is brave enough
to tell you something you said
or did was harmful, take in that
feedback—even if it hurts your
feelings to hear it.

This is how we grow!

All of these things
help make a great ally.

And it's important to know that being an ally doesn't come with a big reward.

The point is making allyship
a part of who you are

every day.

And there are lots of ways
you can do this!

Join a club full of people who are different from you. And join with the intention of listening and learning!

If you know someone whose parents are gay (like us!) and they are getting teased about it, speak up. All families are great!

If you notice someone sitting alone at lunch, invite them to your table.

If you notice someone always gets picked last for teams, pick them first next time!

Allyship is about noticing the problems and then being a part of the solution.

And it's **OK** if you mess up when you're trying.

That's a **MILLION** times better than doing nothing.

Apologize and try again with the knowledge you've gained!

Empower people to be themselves by letting them be heard.

Allyship is a path to make the world a better, more equal, more beautifully diverse place.

Welcome

allyship

to the journey.

Outro
for grownups

OK, so what now? How do we continue this education with the kids in our lives? Here's one, really important suggestion: model it in the grownup world! Explain your allyship, what it looks like, and why you do it to your kids.

It's important to note that while some of this book comes from our experiences as gay people and moms, the majority of this information came from teachings from groundbreaking scholars from all different backgrounds and experiences, including Dr. Tina Opie, Dr. Tiffany Jana, Melinda Briana Epler, and many others.

If every kid (and grownup) was committed to taking action in order to level the playing field for everyone to shine equally, we believe the majority of the world's problems could be solved—reading this book with a kid is getting us one step closer to that goal. Kids are curious and ready to change the world. Thank you for positioning them to do so.

Empowering a generation of kids through diverse storytelling.

 **akidsco.com**

Made to empower.

a kids book about **racism**
by Jelani Memory

a kids book about ANXIETY
by Ross Szabo

a kids book about DISABILITY
by Kristine Napper

a kids book about IMAGINATION
by LEVAR BURTON

a kids book about belonging
by Kevin Carroll

a kids book about failure
by Dr. Laymon Hicks

a kids book about GRATITUDE
by Ben Kenyon

a kids book about LIFE ONLINE
by Dave S. Anderson & Blake Fleischacker

a kids book about body image
by Rebecca Alexander

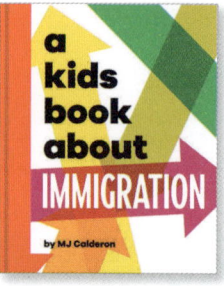
a kids book about IMMIGRATION
by MJ Calderon

a kids book about EMPATHY
by Daron K. Roberts

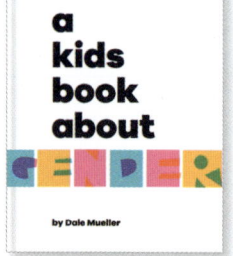
a kids book about GENDER
by Dale Mueller

a kids book about Love
by ZIGGY MARLEY

a kids book about EQUALITY
by BILLIE JEAN KING

a kids book about MONEY
by Adam Stramwasser

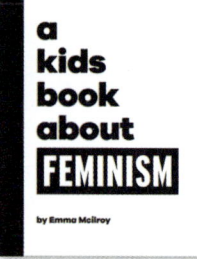
a kids book about FEMINISM
by Emma McIlroy

a kids book about adventure
by Dr. Ben Tertin

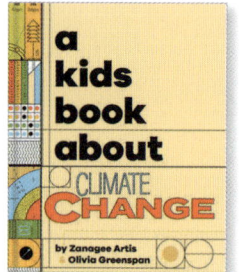
a kids book about CLIMATE CHANGE
by Zanagee Artis & Olivia Greenspan

a kids book about CONFIDENCE
by Joy Cho

a kids book about BEING NONBINARY
by Hunter Chinn-Raicht in partnership with The GenderCool Project

Discover more at akidsco.com